# How to Keep
# Young Children
# Safe

Also available:

**In this series: Health and Safety in Early Years Settings**

*How to Avoid Illness and Infection*
Lynn Parker
1-84312-299-5

*How to Do a Health and Safety Audit*
Lynn Parker
1-84312-303-7

**Other:**

*The A–Z of School Health: A Guide for Teachers*
Adrian Brooke and Steve Welton
1-84312-830-4

# How to Keep Young Children Safe

## Lynn Parker

 **David Fulton** Publishers

David Fulton Publishers Ltd
The Chiswick Centre, 414 Chiswick High Road, London W4 5TF

www.fultonpublishers.co.uk

First published in Great Britain in 2006 by David Fulton Publishers

10 9 8 7 6 5 4 3 2 1

David Fulton Publishers is a division of Granada Learning Limited

*British Library Cataloguing in Publication Data*
A catalogue record for this book is available from the British Library.

ISBN: 1 84312 301 0

Typeset by FiSH Books, Enfield, Middx.
Printed and bound in Great Britain

# Contents

# Foreword

Working with young children is both a pleasure and a privilege, but with each of these comes responsibility. One key area of responsibility is health and safety. Managers of all early years settings need a clear understanding of what is required, both to fulfil their duties, and to impart knowledge to their staff and those training with them. These books will help achieve this.

One of the first things students undertaking training in early years are introduced to is safe practice, both for themselves and for the children they will work with. The importance of taking responsibility for personal safety is discussed in this series along with how to observe and supervise children appropriately. The *Health and Safety in the Early Years* series presents three accessible books covering all the main aspects of health and safety in early years environments under three main topics. These books will be of considerable use to managers, qualified practitioners and students on a range of courses.

The series can be read as a set, perhaps to support assignment work or within staff training, or as stand alone texts. Managers will find examples to help them support the development of their staff, as the books present information that will both consolidate and extend understanding for most readers. Useful chapter summaries and best practice checklists help give an 'at a glance' reminder of what should be happening today and every day. The use of bullet points for emphasis throughout the books works well, and each book includes a comprehensive list of references and/or contacts.

In *How to Keep Young Children Safe* the focus is on keeping children safe in a variety of situations; inside the setting, in the outdoor play space, and on outings. Guidance is also given regarding coping with injuries should they occur.

This series highlights why re-visiting understanding, and updating knowledge of this area of responsibility is so important.

Sandy Green – Early Years Consultant

# Introduction to the series

This book is one of a series of three addressing the issue of health and safety within the early years setting. Those who work with young children have a responsibility for providing a safe environment to ensure their well-being. The National Standards provide a baseline for the provision of quality child care but you also need to comply with national legislation covering health and safety, food hygiene and fire safety.

This book aims to provide practical information on making the indoor and outdoor space a safe environment for children to use throughout the year. Many accidents that happen to children are preventable. By planning ahead certain hazards can be identified and either be removed or reduced to make sure that the number of serious or fatal accidents are minimised.

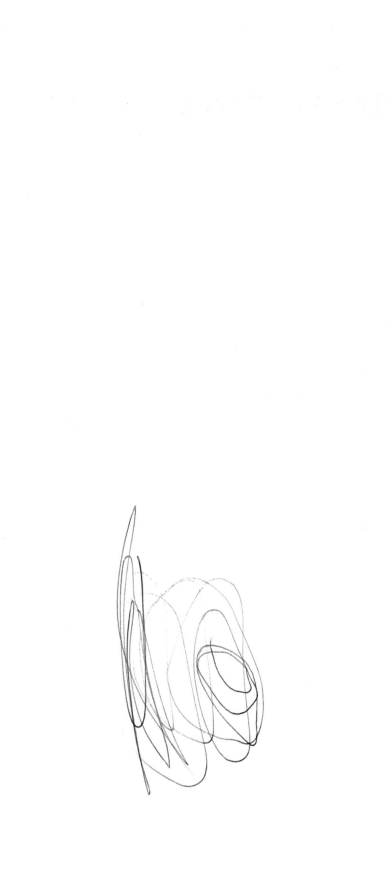

# Key information

## Calling the emergency services

Keep the following information by all telephones in your setting:

Dial 999 (or 112) and request the service needed – fire, ambulance, police.

Provide the following information as asked:

+ telephone number of the setting;

+ postal address including the postcode;

+ the specific location within the setting, e.g. baby room;

+ your name;

+ the nature of the problem – if you need an ambulance give a short description of the child's symptoms along with their name and age;

+ the best entrance to enter the setting and say that someone will meet and direct the emergency crew to the location inside the building;

+ the name of the member of staff nominated to meet the emergency team.

## CHAPTER 1

# Planning for safety

## Introduction

Children are naturally curious and need constant supervision. This is why it is important to assess your setting for risks and to incorporate safety features into your structure, policies and practice. When considering both inside and outside spaces it is important to think of the activities that will be undertaken there. Children experience minor injuries every day, ranging from scratches to bumps and bruises. Most injuries of the minor or indeed more serious type are the result of falls, burns, scalds, poisoning and near drowning. Planning for safety means that everyone has to be involved – including parents and the children themselves.

This chapter provides a template for a suggested safety plan, a self-review activity and a checklist of best practice to consider.

## Planning for safety

### Drawing up a safety plan

You should have a written safety plan to give to parents and carers. This will also provide a reference point for auditing and future development.

There are three main parts to a safety plan:

+ the aim

+ the current situation

+ future plans.

A safety plan should start with a general statement of safety saying what you hope to achieve. The current situation should be described in terms of the:

+ facilities available

+ staff and their different roles and responsibilities

+ equipment available and the standard procedures to be followed for when it is used.

## Action plan

An action plan should be included in the safety plan, with a timetable stating when the future improvements will be made. This will include identifying any gaps in current practices and procedures and how they can be improved. Any list created should be prioritised according to the urgency of the work, the finances available, and restrictions to the facility and the mix of staff if it involves staff training.

Consulting with staff and parents about improvements and how they can be achieved is useful as they often suggest ideas and initiatives that one person on their own might not.

Finally the safety plan should always be reviewed on a regular basis annually and after any incident has occurred.

---

A safety plan should include:

+ general information about the facility;

+ named staff members with responsibility for safety;

+ outline plan of the area;

+ emergency first-aid procedures, named staff member for first aid, where first-aid kits can be found on the premises;

+ procedures for buying, and using equipment under supervision;

+ rules for accepted behaviour by children, families and staff;

+ checklists for maintenance procedures;

+ information on trips and outings away from the premises;

+ education and training programme for children and staff.

---

*Suggested safety plan*

## Outline safety plan

### General information

[Give an introduction to your nursery, who you are and the type of services provided]

### Person responsible for safety

[Include the name of the member of staff responsible for safety and who to contact when that person is not available]

### Outline plan of the area

[Provide a simple drawing of the nursery covering both the inside and outside areas]

### Emergency first-aid procedures

[Include the name of the member of staff who is responsible for first aid, which may be the same person responsible for overall safety. Also include information about where first-aid kits are kept in the nursery and the procedures that will be followed if an accident happens]

### Buying and using equipment

[List the criteria followed when purchasing equipment and the protocol for supervising children when they use such equipment, e.g. a climbing frame]

### Rules for acceptable behaviour by children, families and staff

[State the accepted behaviour and the action that will be taken should it not be followed, this could be linked to your complaints procedure]

### Checklists for maintenance procedures

[State what your policy is on maintenance of equipment and the procedures in place to achieve this]

### Outside trips and outings

[Provide information on the procedures in place when children leave your nursery]

### Education and training programme on safety

[State the type and frequency of education and training provided to staff and how their knowledge is updated, including fire drills, safety talks and general inspections. You may also wish to link this to teaching children about safety by being good role models in everyday activities and using play equipment properly]

## Appointing a safety worker

Under the Health and Safety at Work etc. Act (1974) everyone has a responsibility to maintain a safe working environment but there should be one person with overall responsibility for co-ordinating and making sure that it happens. It is important to be clear about who will manage this responsibility when the named worker is on holiday or off sick.

Even the smallest of early years settings needs to have someone to be named as being specifically responsible for safety.

### Areas of responsibility

The named worker has responsibility for:

+ arranging inspections of the premises on a regular basis;

+ making an inspection after an incident or change has happened;

+ maintaining accident records and organising practice drills for evacuation and fire;

+ maintaining first-aid provision;

+ providing induction training for new staff and annual updates for those staff already employed;

+ providing information to parents of existing safety plans;

+ taking a leadership role in developing, implementing and monitoring safety plans;

+ regularly reviewing the accident records of the facility to identify areas for improvement;

+ arranging and supervising work that needs doing;

+ providing to officials inspecting the premises the safety plan, timeframe for its implementation and any other documentation required.

Once appointed the person responsible for safety should look at the physical environment and the routines in place for maintaining a safe environment.

# The early years environment

## The building

✚ Does the building have to be shared with other organisations?

✚ How much storage space is there and does it have to be shared?

✚ What access do children have to different parts of the premises?

If the building is shared with others you should agree a safety plan for the shared areas. Check that all shared areas comply with your own safety plan before allowing children to access them.

## Safety routines

Safety should be included as part of everyday practices without being seen as something that is extra to the daily routine. It should become second nature for staff to consider the environment in which they work and identify hazards either to themselves, their colleagues or children.

## Routine tasks

### Assessing, monitoring and maintaining safety

Safety checks should be carried out at regular intervals. This includes:

✚ a visual inspection by walking around the premises making sure that safety equipment is in good order and being used;

✚ checking safety gates are in place;

✚ ensuring storerooms are closed and not accessible to children or visitors;

✚ ensuring floors are clear of clutter and are clean and well maintained;

✚ checking all equipment works by physically testing it.

Not everything needs to be checked every day but it is important to draw up a checklist that can be signed and dated to make sure nothing is forgotten. The safety plan should identify what needs to be checked daily, weekly, monthly or yearly. Future dates for inspections should be put in the diary to remind staff when they are to take place, and an independent inspection of the early years setting of premises, equipment and policies should be undertaken. This can be done through Ofsted if you are registered with them but a fee will be required.

## Buying, installing and using equipment

Early years settings should have guidelines for the purchasing, installing and use of new equipment. This ensures that only equipment that complies with current safety laws and standards is purchased and that its use can be included in the safety policy and hygiene policy.

## Access to the early years settings

There should be clear procedures for managing access not only to make sure that children stay on the premises but also to prevent unwanted visitors.

Access can be controlled by:

+ height of handles on doors and locks on windows;

+ use of security systems of alarms, intercoms, name badges, CCTV;

+ promoting staff awareness of other people on the premises of visitors, contractors or other users;

+ information to staff, parents and visitors through posters, notices and leaflets.

Advice can be obtained from the local crime prevention officer about making the premises secure. The fire safety officer can also be contacted to make sure that fire safety requirements are not compromised from any safety measures implemented such as locking doors.

## Security measures

Security measures can include:

+ a system for reporting suspicious incidents;

+ staff reporting strangers on the premises;

+ waste and recycling bins being locked up every night;

+ security lighting at entrances, footpaths and building facades;

+ surveillance system such as CCTV or security patrols;

- use of intruder alarms;

- automated fire detection system;

- marking of property and secure storage of expensive equipment.

Provisions for managing access include:

- having a book that visitors are required to sign on entering the premises, stating the purpose of the visit with arrival and departure times;

- setting up procedures for staff, children, parents and visitors that use identity checks;

- establishing what to do if children are not collected;

- requesting written permission from parents if children are to be picked up by another adult.

## Record keeping

It is very important that accurate and concurrent records are kept whether they are either paper based or on computer. It is important that you have:

- up-to-date contact details for each child, including home phone number, work contact details and where parents or carers are usually based while the child is at your facility;

- accurate details of any medication, medical or physical conditions or allergies that a child may have;

- details of each child's GP and surgery contact details;

- daily register of attendance;

- an accurate record of all accidents that happen to children or staff members, in a special accident record book;

- records of those visiting the premises.

All records should be available for inspection and reviewed on a regular basis. While records are important for insurance purposes they provide you with valuable information.

✚ Review the accident records on a monthly basis to see if any patterns are emerging.

✚ Review the accident records once a year as this gives you a different picture and alternative pattern to the incidents recorded.

If reviewed regularly the records may show that a particular piece of equipment or area of the outdoor play facility is where the majority of accidents are happening or that they are occurring at a certain time of day. Any changes made should be recorded in the accident record book to show that steps have been taken to prevent similar accidents happening again.

## Communication

### Teaching children about safety

You should never expect young children to keep themselves safe, as babies and toddlers have no sense of what is and is not safe. Between the ages of three and five years old children have a limited idea of danger but will forget any instructions you give them if they get excited or upset. What you can do is to teach them by:

✚ setting a good example in everyday activities;

✚ showing them how to use play equipment properly;

✚ repeatedly telling them what is potentially dangerous and why.

Young children do not remember everything you tell them or do as you ask, especially when they get distracted. However, you should reinforce safety messages and good behaviour at every opportunity so that children know what to do, as they grow older.

### Teaching parents and families

Children's parents and families should be included in all your safety messages so that they can understand the reasoning behind what you have put in place and why.

✚ Keep parents aware of your safety practices and their role in helping to maintain these practices.

- Make your safety plan available to them.

- Explain the behaviour expected and why.

- Gain their permission to take their child to hospital in case of an emergency.

- Demonstrate the use of any safety equipment you may have.

- Actively involve parents and families in any first-aid courses you run and provide them with accident prevention leaflets.

## Teaching staff

Your safety plan should form the basis of standard training for all staff. All staff should be kept informed and up-to-date with any changes to the safety plan. Accident prevention should be kept in the forefront of everybody's mind by having regular safety talks and general inspections.

## Best practice checklist

- Have a safety plan.

- Appoint a safety worker.

- Have an independent inspection of the premises carried out annually.

- Have secure systems in place for managing access to the premises.

- Have guidelines for purchasing new equipment.

- Know what to do if children are not collected by their parents.

- Provide induction training and annual updates for staff.

- Keep accurate records of accidents, inspections and maintenance.

**SELF-REVIEW ACTIVITY**

Look at the suggested safety outline plan on page 3 and considering your own premises:

✚ Compare it to your own current safety plan.

   – Does your plan cover similar or different topics; if the latter how does it differ and why?

   – Have you got rules for behaviour of staff, children, parents and visitors to the premises and how were they decided?

   – What is your policy for access to the premises?

   – What do you do if someone other than the child's parent comes to collect them or no one turns up?

✚ If you have not got a safety plan use the suggested outline and draw up your own safety plan.

✚ Consider the training provided for staff and how it can be improved.

## End-of-chapter summary

This chapter has considered the importance of drawing up a safety plan for early years settings and appointing a safety officer to make sure that the premises comply with the Standard 6 of the National Standards that focuses on ensuring that appropriate safety measures are taken to avoid dangerous situations. This includes assessing security of the premises and making sure that children stay on the premises.

# Safety inside the early years setting

## Introduction

Unlike the outdoors, which is often considered to be a dangerous place, indoors is thought of as being safe and secure. However, children under five years old commonly experience accidents indoors and it is not the place of safety imagined by adults. The implications for the early years setting mean that the hazards children need to be protected against must be identified and actions taken to keep them to a minimum. This chapter looks at the hazardous areas that can be found inside the early years setting and discusses the ways that risks are reduced.

## Moving around safely

### Hazardous areas

While a purpose-built facility is the ideal, a number of early years settings are conversions of residential property or are used by other organisations. As such there are areas in buildings that children should not have access to and these include:

+ cellars

+ attics

+ garages

+ roofs

+ sheds

+ balconies.

Alongside such areas you should think carefully about where children regularly go to as well as the main rooms. This can include corridors to and from exits or to the toilets, garden or outside area.

### Stairs, steps and flooring

The most common area for children, especially those under five years old, to have accidents is on the stairs, steps and flooring.

+ Older buildings are more likely to have uneven steps, open risers, spiral staircases.

+ Banister spacing should not be wider than 10 cm or 6.5 cm if babies are cared for and any horizontal banister spacing should be boarded in as children can easily climb them.

+ Babies and young children should always be supervised when on the stairs and safety gates fitted to restrict access to these areas. Safety gates should always be kept closed and children and adults should not be allowed to climb over them.

+ The stairs should be checked for wear and tear and immediate repairs made to any loose carpet or treads.

+ Consider what is at the bottom of the stairs as it could cause serious injury, such as radiators, furniture, glass doors, etc. Radiators may be moved or covered, furniture could be moved, glass doors should be replaced if at all possible.

+ Floors should be kept as clean as possible but not be over-polished so they cause slips.

+ Mats placed on the floor should be fixed, to avoid the risk of slips and trips.

+ Regularly check floors for wear and tear.

+ Make sure floors are even and any changes in height are well defined, such as steps, terraces, ramps etc.

### Doors and windows

+ Doors should be fitted with safety devices wherever possible to stop children from trapping their fingers.

- Doorways should be kept clear of furniture and equipment especially if they are emergency or fire exit doors.

- Child-resistant locks should be fitted to windows and any keys should be kept out of reach of children.

- Safety glass should be fitted in doors and low windows.

- Furniture that can be used by children to climb on should not be placed below windows.

### Bathrooms and toilets

- Hot taps should be fitted with a thermostatic mixing valve (TMV).

- There should be grab rails and slip-resistant finishes or mats in showers and baths.

- Bathrooms and toilets should be able to be unlocked from the outside.

### Equipment and furniture

- Any furniture or equipment that is attached to the wall should be secure and stable.

- Children should be discouraged from climbing onto furniture.

- Equipment such as high chairs needs to be fitted with five-point harnesses.

- Check all equipment, furniture, fixture and fittings on a regular basis for wear and tear and replace when necessary.

- Be aware of sharp corners on furniture and equipment that is at eye level for young children.

### Storage areas

- Potentially dangerous equipment such as scissors and craft knives should be stored out of reach of children and kept in drawers or cupboards that are fitted with child-resistant locks.

- Store cupboards should be kept locked and not be accessible to children.

- Store equipment safely in a stable condition so stacked items do not fall onto staff or children.

*Kitchens*

✚ Children should not have access to areas where hot and cold food or drinks are prepared.

✚ Children should be taught how to use utensils safely.

✚ Hot drinks should not be allowed near young children.

## Specific indoor areas

### Space and facility requirements

There are specific space and facility requirements under *The Children Act 1989* for early years settings. These include the following:

✚ Group size is never bigger than 26 children, though early years settings can have more than one group.

✚ Premises are clean, well lit, with natural lighting, ventilated and maintained in a good state of repair and decoration.

✚ There is access to a telephone on the premises.

✚ Rooms are maintained at an appropriate temperature.

✚ The premises are for the sole use of the early years setting during the hours they are open.

✚ The indoor play area has the minimum space per child of
   – under 2 years old – 3.5 square metres
   – 2 years old – 2.5 square metres
   – 3–7 years old – 2.3 square metres.

✚ A kitchen equipped to give meals and snacks for children and staff on the premises conforms to environmental health and food safety regulations.

✚ There is a staff room or area separate from areas used by children.

✚ There are separate laundry facilities which are not accessible to children.

### Toilet and hand washing facilities

✚ There is a minimum of one toilet and one hand wash basin with hot and cold water for every ten children over two years old.

+ There are child-size toilets and hand wash basins as they reduce accidents and promote independence.

+ Hot water taps should have thermostatic mixer valves fitted.

+ A separate room or partitioned area is available for nappy changing.

+ There are separate toilet facilities for adults.

+ If toilet doors have locks fitted they should be able to be opened from both sides.

## Rest and sleep facilities

+ There is a partitioned area or separate room that is warm, well ventilated, with curtains and dimly lit.

+ There should be quiet, calm conditions conducive to rest and sleep.

+ Cots should be spaced at 18 inches to 3 foot (45–90 cm) apart to reduce the risk of cross-infection between children.

+ Clean bedding should be supplied for each child.

+ Children must always be supervised whether inside or outside when sleeping.

## Safety standards for toys and play equipment

All toys or play equipment have a suggested age range on the packaging and this reflects the manufacturer's view of the age group that they believe will find the toy most appealing. If a warning symbol states a toy is not suitable for any child under the age of 36 months it should not be purchased as it may contain parts that could choke a young child. Other symbols include:

+ European Standard BS EN 71 showing that the toy has been tested to agreed safety standards.

+ CE mark which is a legal requirement for all toys sold in the European Union.

+ Lion Mark which is used by members of the British Toy and Hobby Association.

If you think any toy, whether purchased from a shop or homemade, is unsafe then it should not be used in the early years setting.

+ Toys should be made of good quality materials with non-toxic paints and plastic rounded corners and edges.

+ Any toys that start to show wear and tear and are damaged should be thrown away.

+ Toys with strings or cords that are longer than 30 cm (12 inches) should not be available as such cords can easily wrap around the neck of a child.

## Choosing appropriate toys

Toys and play equipment should be chosen to develop a child's social, emotional, cognitive and physical skills.

It is important to remember to avoid toys that have:

+ sharp points;

+ jagged edges;

+ rough surfaces;

+ small detachable or insecure parts that can be swallowed or stuck in the throat, nose or ears;

+ sharp spikes or pins that could injure if the toy is pulled apart;

+ long cords or strings more than 30 cms (12 inches).

Also avoid:

+ caps, guns or toys that make large noises that could damage hearing;

+ computer games and videos with flickering lights that may trigger fits in children with epilepsy.

Further toy safety information can be found in Chapter 5.

## Other equipment hazards

### Changing tables

There are different types of changing tables:

+ wooden with guardrails

+ fold-up models

+ hinged chest adapters.

**Warning!**

*Hinged chest adapters are not recommended as there have been reports of them toppling over when babies have been placed on them near the outer edge.*

When considering what type of changing table to purchase you should:

+ check the sturdiness of fold-up models when they are open;

+ consider a table with shelves and compartments for storing equipment in;

+ have a guardrail that is 5 cm (2 inches) high on wooden changing tables.

### Dummies, rattles, squeeze toys, teething rings

A risk of choking to babies and toddlers can be associated with these items and other objects that can be put into the mouth. Items that are the most risk are those that have handles or small ends that can be placed in the mouth.

+ Do not leave babies or toddlers with any small object in their cot when they are sleeping.

+ Do not fasten teething rings, dummies or rattles around a baby's neck.

### Toy chests

Accidents have been reported of young children reaching over and into toy chests and the lids falling onto their head or necks. Another potentially fatal, but less frequent, hazard is suffocation when children climb into the toy chest to hide.

If used you should:

+ buy toy chests that have detachable lids or doors;

+ look for toy chests that have ventilation holes that will not be blocked, or have a gap between the lid and the sides of the chest;

+ make sure the lid does not have a latch.

### Hook-on chairs

These are used as substitutes for high chairs and are attached to the edge of the table. There are reports of children falling out of them or them becoming dislodged from the table.

If used you should:

+ not place the chair where the child's feet can push against the table, chair or supports and dislodge it from the table;

+ ensure that the restraining straps are used and fastened securely around the child;

+ never leave a child unattended when in the chair;

+ never use these types of chair on glass-top, single pedestal or on unstable tables.

## Safety equipment

While safety equipment might help prevent a number of accidents, it is no substitute for supervision.

### Safety gates

These are designed to prevent access to potentially hazardous areas by toddlers and young children. They are often seen at the top and bottom of stairs but can also be used to keep children in a single room. There are gates that have extensions so that they can fit wider-than-average corridors and doorways.

### Fire guards

These can be fitted to heaters and radiators to reduce the risk of accidental burns for children and adults. They should be suitable for the heater but it is important to make sure that they have no contact with the heater and are at least 20 cms from the heat source or the guard itself will then become dangerously hot and become the risk.

### Smoke alarms

All homes should have smoke alarms fitted and buildings open to the public should have fire alarms fitted that are tested weekly. The Fire Safety Officer will be able to provide detailed information about what is necessary for the individual early years setting.

### Fire blanket

This is standard equipment in the kitchen area and should be fixed to the wall near the cooker. All staff should know how to use it.

### Fire extinguishers

These should be checked and serviced regularly and staff should be trained how to use them. The Fire Safety Officer provides information on the most appropriate type of extinguisher for the premises.

### Thermostatic mixing valves

These should be fitted to all hot water taps to avoid scalding. It is always best to put cold water into the bath first and then to add the hot. You should always test the bath water with your elbow before bathing a child whether a thermostatic mixing valve is used or not.

## Window locks

These allow windows to be opened wide enough for ventilation but not wide enough for a child to squeeze through. Locks should be appropriate for the type of window and fitted following the instructions.

## Cupboard and drawer catches

Fitted to cupboards and drawers these help to contain potentially dangerous equipment such as scissors and knives. However, there are some young children who are able to open these catches.

## Playpens

While not strictly classed as safety equipment, these do serve a function for keeping babies and toddlers in one place. They should be regularly checked as part of a maintenance programme. Slat spaces on a wooden playpen should be no more than 60 mm apart and playpens with a hinge in the centre of the top rails should automatically lock when they are lifted into the normal use position.

## Five-point harnesses

These should be used for babies and toddlers when they are in high chairs or prams but should not be left dangling when not in use as children could get caught up in the straps.

# Best practice checklist

✚ Identify hazardous areas in the premises and also those areas where children should not be allowed access, e.g. store rooms, kitchens etc.

✚ Ensure the fixtures and fittings are made safe by having safety glass in doors and low windows.

✚ Assess the furniture and equipment to make it child-friendly.

✚ Keep storage areas secure.

✚ Children should not have access to kitchen and food preparation areas.

✚ Room sizes and usage should conform to Standard 4 for physical environment. (Standard 4 is one of the National Standards that Ofsted inspect against and refers to the standard for the physical environment which requires you to: make sure the premises are safe, secure and suitable for their purpose. That they provide adequate space in an appropriate location, are welcoming to children and offer access to the necessary facilities for a range of activities which promote their development (DfES 2003).)

✚ Fit child-size toilets and hand wash basins to promote independence.

✚ Provide suitable rest and sleep facilities.

✚ Only use toys that conform to current safety standards and are appropriate for the age of the child.

✚ Use safety equipment to reduce accidents where appropriate, such as safety gates etc.

---

**SELF-REVIEW ACTIVITY**

Consider the inside of your early years setting. What hazardous areas can you identify and what safety precautions could you suggest to prevent accidents?

You may consider:

✚ the kitchen and food preparation areas

✚ toilet and nappy changing areas

✚ corridors and stairs

✚ improving lighting levels in corridors and stairs

✚ keeping corridors, doorways and stairs free of equipment

✚ cleaning up spillages as soon as possible

✚ using safety gates where appropriate

✚ using harnesses for babies in high chairs and prams.

---

## End-of-chapter summary

The physical environment inside early years settings can have an impact on safety. Children need to explore and experiment with their surroundings but there should be a balance between this need and a safe environment. This chapter has tried to identify some of the hazards that can be encountered inside early years settings and provide information on safety equipment that may be used to help to reduce such risks. By having systems in place, safety practices can be incorporated into daily routines and potential hazards quickly identified.

# Safety outside the early years setting

## Introduction

Within the curriculum outdoor play is an important part of young children's education. The outside is a natural place for children to be which is enjoyable, fun and where they can be uninhibited and have a sense of freedom (Bilton 2004).

Health and safety has often been the reason given by early years settings for not using the outdoor space. This chapter looks at how areas and activities can be managed safely to ensure that children have an opportunity to discover the outdoors.

## Play and activity areas

When designing outdoor play areas there are numerous things to consider for achieving maximum safety. These include simple things like making sure there is enough shade so that children can play out of direct sunlight and that the area can be clearly seen from other areas of the child care facility to assist with supervision. The play areas should be enclosed with childproof fencing to guard against stray dogs entering the area and to prevent the children from wandering out into the local neighbourhood and onto roads.

## Toddler areas

For babies and toddlers there should be a separate play space that allows them to crawl safely with age-appropriate equipment such as climbing frames, slides, swings, ramps, tunnels and wheeled toys. It is essential that this young age group are closely supervised to prevent accidents and injuries.

For babies, if possible there should be an area where prams can be placed so that they can sleep and rest outside where it is sheltered.

## Playgrounds

In the UK in 1999 over 150,000 children were injured in school or nursery playgrounds. There is one fatal accident every three to four years (LAC 79/2 (2002)) on average. These accidents happen in public playgrounds, parks, schools and public houses or restaurants. The play equipment most commonly involved in accidents were:

+ climbing frames

+ swings

+ slides.

Other equipment involved in accidents included rope swings, seesaws and roundabouts.

### Where to site the play area

Managers of early years settings should think about where the play area is sited and ensure that any equipment is properly designed and installed and maintained. The management systems in place should make sure that the area is maintained in good order and that any damage is repaired quickly. If the play area is already well established, a risk assessment should be carried out and the results used so that an improvement programme can be drawn up, with priorities being identified to cover renewal, refurbishment or removal of equipment, and consider installing impact absorbing surfaces (IAS) as part of the assessment process.

### Installing or refurbishing play areas

When installing or refurbishing existing play areas it is important to make sure that they meet the requirements of the EN Standards (European Standards – for more detail consult the British Standards Institution www.bsi-global.com). A risk assessment should be carried out on the play area that includes both the EN Standards and health and safety legislation.

*European Standards*

There are two European Standards relevant to safety in children's play areas. BS EN 1176 covers the requirements for design, manufacture and installation of play area equipment. BS EN 1177 states what surfaces should be used in the play area and methods for testing. The standards are not retrospective and are not legally binding but early years settings should know about them and take them into consideration when making decisions about play areas and equipment.

*Inspection of play areas*

Inspections of play areas must be carried out by a competent person which can be someone who is registered with the Register of Play Inspectors International Ltd (RPII). Inspectors will be looking for the following to be in place:

+ management systems

+ risk assessments

+ action plan and a timescale for action

+ priority for the action areas of concern.

Following the inspection, enforcement action could be considered if there are no management systems, an absence of action plans or if timescales for action are unreasonably long, and if there is no IAS in the impact area.

## Different surfaces

Impact absorbing surfacing (IAS) covers a wide range of materials including manufactured tiles, loose particulates and natural materials such as turf, bark and sand.

Installing these surfaces is not the complete answer to preventing injuries in a playground. IAS are tested for their efficacy in reducing the severity of head injuries so they may not be effective in reducing other types of injuries.

*Paths, paving and stairs*

Any paving and stairs should be made of non-slip material, with handrails and appropriate protective barriers. Repairs should be made as soon as possible to uneven paving slabs and broken concrete to stop children and staff from tripping or falling over. Paths should also be kept clear of mud, and moss-covered paths or patio areas should be cleared as quickly as possible. Chairs and tables should be stacked and stored away and not be accessible to children.

## Water

Whether water is held in a garden pond, rainwater butt, paddling pool or a bucket, a young child will go and investigate due to their natural inquisitiveness. Drowning in the garden is the third largest cause of accidental death in the home for the under-fives over the last decade. However, it seems that children are up to 80 per cent more likely to drown in someone else's garden, such as neighbours, relatives and friends.

Due to the dangers, early years settings do not usually have ponds, but if you are working in an environment where there is one you should consider the safety advice below.

## Children most at risk of drowning

Children need to be closely supervised at all times in and around water with those most at risk being the under-fives, especially one- and two-year-olds, with boys accounting for 78 per cent of incidents in the UK. The main water features involved are:

+ garden ponds

+ swimming and paddling pools

+ other water containers.

### Pond safety

Ponds are not safe, and are very rarely used in dedicated early years settings. Even the shallowest of ponds, from a child's perspective, can be lethal, with a 500 mm deep pond equivalent to an adult falling into 1800 mm of water, the difference being that the child would be unable to climb out of the water. If you do work in a location where a pond is present, and cannot be filled in, there is something you can do.

Ponds can be made safer by good design. Ponds should be covered with a grill that should be able to support the weight of a child and be above the surface of the water at all times. Modular interlocking plastic grids that can be made to fit various shapes and sizes of ponds are available, as well as steel mesh. The mesh should be heavy duty (i.e. 6–8 mm diameter wire) and be self-supporting, and have a grid size of no more than 80 mm x 80 mm to prevent a child becoming trapped. Any method used to secure and lock the frame in place should make sure that there is no risk of children trapping themselves between any moving parts.

Simply fencing off a pond is not good enough. It is only a partial solution and could lead to a false sense of security. Gates can be accidentally left open, and children at three years of age can climb an unsuitable fence within 30 seconds.

## Alternatives to ponds

✦ Paddling pools have long been popular but children should never be left unsupervised when they are used and they should always be emptied after use then turned upside down so that rainwater cannot accumulate.

✦ In summer weather sprinklers are a popular alternative; there are now specific child-friendly sprinklers in the shapes of flowers or animals.

## Sandpits

Sandpits are a popular outdoor activity.

They should be placed in partial shade, be well drained and the borders rounded and covered when not in use. Formed plastic sand boxes are best as they are light enough to remove and replace. Sand used in sandpits should be specifically purchased for use to ensure it is not contaminated and should be replaced on a regular basis and kept securely covered so that animals cannot use it as a toilet area.

# Having a wildlife garden

Wildlife gardens are increasingly popular as a way of introducing children to the natural world by studying it using informal and curriculum activities and by practical care of the garden.

## Garden plants

Poisoning by plants in the UK is rare but it is important to have knowledge of any plants that may cause harm to young children. The Royal Horticultural Society and other horticultural organisations have compiled a list of potentially harmful plants and have developed a Code of Recommended Retail Practice for labelling plants at garden centres and nurseries.

Many plants, including their fruit and seeds, are safe and good to eat and are recognised as food plants. Most plants found in the home and gardens are ornamental plants or weeds that are not dangerous.

Small children often like to nibble plants and need to be taught not to eat any part of a growing plant. A sensible rule is to make sure that children know not to eat anything that is not recognised as food.

## Allergic reaction to plants

As well as the dangers of eating poisonous plants there is the possibility of suffering an irritant or allergic reaction through contact with a plant or its sap.

There are three main types of contact hazards:

✚ A burning sensation and sometimes blistering of the skin can affect anyone if they have sufficient exposure to irritant sap.

✚ Some individuals who acquire sensitivity to plants that contain chemicals called allergens can suffer an allergic reaction. Often this presents as dermatitis but in some people it can be a more intense reaction, such as seen in nut allergies.

✚ A few plants have sap that makes the skin sensitive to strong sunlight. Consequently, contact with this type of plant followed by exposure to strong sunlight causes a very severe localised sunburn with blistering and a long-lasting skin discolouration.

## First aid

If you think a child has eaten part of a doubtful plant you should:

✚ seek medical advice at once from a hospital accident and emergency department;

✚ take a sample of the plant so that it can be identified;

✚ not make any attempt to make the child be sick;

In cases of irritant or allergic dermatitis, contact a doctor and take a sample of the plant with you.

---

### Common names of some poisonous plants

| | |
|---|---|
| Autumn crocus | Hellebores (Christmas rose, Lenten rose) |
| Bluebell | Iris |
| Calla lily | Ivy |
| Cuckoo-pint (lords and ladies) | Laburnum |
| Daphne | Lily of the valley |
| Deadly nightshade | Mandrake |
| Delphinium | Monkshood |
| Euphorbia | Wisteria |
| Foxglove | |

---

### *Ideas for a child-friendly garden*

✚ Grow a herb wheel along with fast-growing salad crops that can be eaten.

✚ Make a bog garden using an old washing-up bowl.

✚ Have a bubble fountain instead of a pond.

✚ Make an insect corner with a pile of logs in a shady corner to attract insets.

✚ Have a planting and growing area, using plant pots, tubs, troughs and growbags.

✚ Have a bird feeding station and put out different types of food to attract a range of birds.

## Fences and hedges

Any fencing, while useful, can cause concern as young children may try to climb over it. If it is made of wire they can cut their hands and feet. Hedges can be hazardous to the eyes.

## Insect bites and stings

### *Bees, hornets and wasps*

These insects have small sacs of venom that are designed to hurt and drive off intruders. They are attracted to bright clothing and strong-smelling soaps and perfumes. If they land on you or the children stand still and do not run away or try to hit them, as they will just get agitated.

If they do sting, immediately check whether the child has an allergy to stings – usually known as anaphylaxis.

 *Anaphylaxis is an extreme allergic reaction that can be life threatening and needs urgent medical treatment.*

*What are the signs and symptoms of anaphylaxis?*

Each child is different and the signs and symptoms appear almost immediately after being exposed to an allergen and include some or all of the following:

+ swelling of the face, throat, tongue and lips

+ a metallic taste or itching in the mouth

+ difficulty in swallowing

+ flushed complexion

+ abdominal cramps and nausea

+ increased pulse rate

+ wheezing or difficulty in breathing

+ collapse or unconsciousness

+ widespread red, blotchy skin eruptions

+ puffiness around the eyes.

*Practical guidance*

+ If the child has an adrenaline pen, and staff are trained and permission given, administer the device.

+ If the child collapses or falls unconscious, place them in the recovery position and remain with them until help arrives (be prepared to resuscitate if required).

+ Call an ambulance immediately if there is any doubt about the severity of the reaction or if the child does not respond to medication.

Keep adrenaline pens easily available to staff and always carry them on trips and visits.

If the child is not known to be allergic you should still watch for signs of a reaction but you can make the child more comfortable by checking the site of the sting closely, and if the stinger is still in place, gently scraping it out with a credit card or other blunt-edged item. Apply a cold compress to reduce any swelling.

## Poisons and chemicals

Other hazards include poisons and chemicals, which should be stored and locked in a secure area with childproof doors. Children's toys should not be stored in the same area or near poisons and chemicals and should be stored well away from all dangerous items that are used outdoors such as power tools and garden tools. Remember never to pour chemicals into soft drinks bottles, as they should be kept in their original containers so they can be identified and handled correctly.

# Outdoor play equipment

There is a wide variety of play equipment available for outdoor activities including:

+ climbing frames

+ timber structures

+ balancing bars

+ slides

+ seesaws.

For toddlers and babies play equipment can include:

+ ramps

+ low slides

+ tunnels.

Trampolines are not suitable for use by toddlers and very young children. Mini-trampettes are popular in early years setting and are an alternative, though children must be supervised at all times by an adult when they are used. No more than one child should use them at any one time.

## Storage of outdoor equipment

Always store equipment away tidily after use to reduce the risk of anyone slipping or tripping up on it. This includes tables and chairs so that children cannot climb onto them and injure themselves. Garden sheds are tempting places for children to explore and children should never have unsupervised access to them; they should always be locked when not in use.

## Sun safety

There is increasing awareness of the dangers as well as the benefits of being exposed to the sun. Infants' skin is sensitive and easily burns because it is thinner and has undeveloped melanin, especially when exposed directly to the sun, the effect of which is increased when it is windy. As a result of excessive heat children can also suffer from heatstroke, which may be accompanied by sunburn. Very young children are not able to control their temperature in the same way as older children and adults, making them more prone to heatstroke.

Early exposure to the sun, especially when it is reflected off the sand and sea, can cause skin cancer in later life. All skin types (Asian, African, Caucasian and mixed race) need protection from the sun by using sunscreen and protective clothing. You should have parents' permission to apply sunscreen – otherwise keep the child out of the sun. Remember that sunscreen products are only as good as the person who is using them! Follow these suggestions:

+ Stay out of the sun when it is at its strongest. This varies and can be a short period from 11am to 2pm or anywhere between 10am and 4pm.

+ The face and neck are the areas most affected by skin cancer from too much sunlight. Wearing wide-brimmed hats or hats with a neck protector is advised.

+ Cover up the body as much as possible by wearing long-sleeved tops and baggy shorts.

+ The minimum sun protection factor (SPF) recommended is 15.

+ The SPF number refers to how much it enhances an individual's natural sun protection – if you normally burn within 20 minutes, using a sunscreen of SPF 15 would protect you for 300 minutes (20 x 15 = 300).

+ Most sunscreens work by absorbing ultraviolet rays but some reflect the rays. Ones that protect against both UVA and UVB are the best. Sunscreens should be used to help protect against sunlight, not as a substitute for avoiding exposure.

+ Some suntanning lotions do not contain sunscreen and will provide no protection.

+ Babies under six months old should be shielded from the sun or wear protective clothing if they have to go out in the sun. Sunscreen is not enough.

+ You can get sunburnt on cloudy or hazy days.

+ After applying sunscreen wait for 20–30 minutes for it to dry and stay on your skin as it takes this long for the chemicals to start working.

+ Reapply waterproof sunscreen every two hours and after being in water.

+ A lotion of milky gel-type sunscreen is preferable to use with young children rather than clear alcohol-type products.

+ Remember the slogan of SLIP, SLAP, SLOP. Slip on some clothes. Slap on a hat. Slop on sunscreen.

## Heatstroke

We are all susceptible to suffering from heatstroke but too much sun can be especially serious for young children as they have difficulty in regulating their own body temperature.

Those who suffer heatstroke will:

+ be flushed and feel hot to touch;

+ have a fever and rapid pulse;

+ be dehydrated;

+ be confused and disorientated and have unco-ordinated movements.

Some children may be nauseous or vomit.

Serious cases of heatstroke can result in hospitalisation and the individual may fall into a coma and die. If a child is suspected of having heatstroke:

+ they must be seen by a doctor;

+ keep them in a cool shaded place;

+ remove any excessive clothing;

+ encourage them to drink cool fluids;

+ increase the ventilation by opening the windows or using a fan;

+ cool the skin by bathing in cool, not cold, water (15–18°C).

## General rules for children

General rules need to be taught to children about health and safety outdoors and certain procedures followed:

+ Make sure that hats and sunscreen are worn in sunny weather to avoid sunstroke and burning.

+ Make sure they drink water regularly to avoid dehydration.

+ Always supervise young children especially when there is water around.

+ Teach children to regularly wash their hands especially after they have handled soil and pets.

+ Stop children sucking their fingers or biting their nails while outside in the garden.

+ Clear any cat or dog mess up before children dig in the ground.

+ Teach the basic rules about handling gardening tools that they can use, and about those that are dangerous to them.

+ Keep garden sheds locked using child locks.

+ Teach children not to touch any dangerous chemicals.

+ Be aware that some plants:
    - can be poisonous, such as berries;
    - can burn the skin or sting, such as stinging nettles;
    - have thorns and hooks, such as roses;
    - have leaves that can cut the skin, such as pampas grass.

## Best practice checklist

+ Make sure play area surfaces are safe, appropriate and conform to recognised safety standards.

+ Check children's outerwear does not have hood or neck drawstrings that could cause strangulation if caught in equipment.

+ Look for safe playground equipment that conforms to a recognised safety standard.

+ Have separate areas for different age groups so that they use age-appropriate equipment.

+ Use impact absorbing surfaces under equipment above 0.6 m in height.

+ Always supervise children closely to avoid injuries.

+ Have a maintenance programme in place and have regular inspections.

+ Keep the area free from clutter, litter and debris.

+ Create a number of play opportunities such as imaginative play, open play, quiet areas and adventurous play.

+ Make sure fences and walls are in good repair.

+ Keep all gates closed.

+ Have safety rules in place that everyone knows and follows.

**SELF-REVIEW ACTIVITY**

Safety can often be seen in negative terms but children need to learn to explore the outside world.

✚ Decide the activities that you would wish young children to experience as part of the early years curriculum outdoors.

✚ Carry out a risk assessment of the outside area and identify any dangers that can be removed.

✚ Draw up safety rules for children and staff to follow so that the activities you have chosen can be undertaken in a safe manner.

You may consider the following:

✚ Can the outside area be divided into zones, areas etc.?

✚ Are equipment and resources stored safely?

✚ Are children involved in setting up and tidying away?

✚ Is children's clothing and footwear suitable for the outdoors, whatever the weather?

✚ Are staffing levels appropriate so that children are closely supervised and supported in all the activities you have provided?

✚ Have safety practices been discussed with the children so they understand the safety rules.

## End-of-chapter summary

Education outdoors is an important part of the early years curriculum and this chapter has discussed the ways in which the outside play area can be made safe for children to use. The use of impact absorbing surfaces and purchasing and upgrading equipment to current safety standards reduces the risk of accidents along with carrying out risk assessment and inspections on a regular basis. While a good design will provide an ideal space to use, it is the level and quality of observation and supervision given to children while they use such space that will ensure they suffer no more severe injury than a scrape to the knee or hand.

## CHAPTER 4

# Preparing for outings and trips

## Introduction

Whether an outing is informal, to local shops and amenities, or is more structured, to farms or local nature reserves, while providing a valuable learning experience it can also bring an increased risk of accidents. It is possible to reduce such risks by meticulous planning and organisation. This chapter considers the planning needed for successful educational visits outside of the early years setting.

## Educational visits

Outings and trips provide opportunities for young children to experience the outdoors in a way not possible in the classroom, and are fun. Careful planning including risk assessment, exploratory visit to the area, first aid, transport and emergency procedures achieve a successful outing. Local education authorities (LEAs) in some areas set their own levels of supervision for visits while others expect this to be done as part of the risk assessment process. Popular outings and trips include visits to the coast, farms, museums, local parks, the high street, the local wood or nature reserve.

## Planning for an educational visit

Guidance for planning educational visits was published by the Department of Education and Skills (DfES). When organising an outing or trip you should consider the:

+ objective of the visit

+ date, venue, length of visit

+ staff to children ratio

+ resources needed

+ estimate of costs

+ appropriate insurance.

Planning should also include:

+ contacting the venue to assess its suitability for young children;

+ deciding what transport is required;

+ deciding who will lead the group;

+ undertaking a risk assessment of the trip and an exploratory visit to the venue;

+ gaining written parental consent;

+ making emergency arrangements;

+ making contingency plans for late return.

### Adult to child ratio

The following ratios usually apply:

✚ 1:1 for children under one year of age

✚ 1:2 for children between one and two years old

✚ 1:3 for children between three and five years old.

### First-aid arrangements

All staff should know about the first-aid arrangements and how to contact the emergency services. A fully qualified first-aider must be on the outing. The minimum first-aid provision for a visit should be:

✚ an adequate first-aid box;

✚ appointing someone to be in charge of the first-aid arrangements;

✚ consideration of the number of children in the group and the activity;

✚ consideration of the type of injuries that might happen and how effective first aid is likely to be;

✚ establishing where the nearest hospital with an accident and emergency department is.

### Travel first-aid box

The minimum contents of a travel first-aid box should be:

✚ a leaflet with general first-aid advice;

✚ six individually wrapped sterile adhesive dressings;

✚ one large sterile unmedicated wound dressing 18 cm x 18 cm;

✚ two triangular bandages;

✚ two safety pins;

✚ individually wrapped moist cleansing wipes;

✚ one pair of disposable gloves.

A resusciade (for hygienic mouth-to-mouth resuscitation) is useful to include.

## Travel arrangements

+ Local education authority regulations should be checked in advance of any outing.

+ All vehicles must have a current MOT certificate of roadworthiness and be taxed and insured.

+ All drivers must have a driving licence that covers the type of vehicle they are driving.

+ All minibuses must have forward-facing seats with seat belts, either lap belts or three-point lap and diagonal belts.

+ Children under three years old must use a child restraint and not an adult seat belt.

+ Child restraints include baby seats, child seats, booster seats and booster cushions (these are manufactured according to different weight ranges).

+ National Standards require that records are kept on vehicles that children are transported in including insurance details and a list of named drivers.

### *Planning the trip (see p. 40)*

+ Check out where you are going to visit.

+ Identify a person responsible for the trip before you go.

+ Obtain parental permission.

+ Tell the children and give them instructions they will understand for their age.

+ Make sure the adult to child ratio is sufficient.

+ Make sure that any equipment or luggage is stored correctly.

+ Leave details of the route and the expected time of return with the early years setting.

✚ Make a list of all who are on the trip and their emergency contact details.

✚ Have an emergency contingency plan ready that includes getting in touch with parents, evacuation of the vehicle, first-aid requirements and what to do if you are going to be returning late.

## On the day of the trip

✚ Make sure that the adults and children know who is responsible for whom.

✚ Make sure that staff members know the procedure should an emergency arise.

✚ Have a list of everyone in the group, both adults and children.

✚ Make regular checks that the whole group is present.

✚ Ensure all children are easily identifiable (badges can be used with the name of the early years setting and emergency contact telephone number).

✚ Avoid identification of children that could put them at risk, e.g. name badges, consider coloured caps or armbands instead.

✚ Make sure that children know what to do if they become separated from the group.

✚ Get children to use a 'buddy' system, so that each regularly checks that the other is OK. (A variation is the 'circle buddy' system where they form a circle and have a left- and right-side buddy.)

✚ Make sure that children wear their seat belts when travelling.

✚ Ensure head counts are carried out when getting on or off transport.

✚ Keep an eye on the weather.

✚ Always have an alternative plan (plan B) in case the itinerary needs to be changed.

## Local outings

Casual trips to places in the local environment near the early years setting can be organised, but as with trips further afield, careful planning makes for a successful outing.

Such outings include trips to:

+ the fire station

+ the greengrocer's shop

+ the park

+ the wood

+ the canal basin

+ the museum

+ the art gallery.

These local outings allow children to explore their own community but any proposed outing should be reviewed for its suitability and whether it is child-friendly and what the learning potentials are for the children.

Whatever the type of visit, whether to a local amenity or further afield to farms or the seaside, the same safety checks need to be undertaken as identified earlier in the chapter.

## Farm visits

The highlight of visiting farms for children is to see the animals, especially lambs, kids, calves and foals, and if possible to touch them. All animals carry a number of microbes as do humans, some of which can be transmitted to us and cause illness. Some of these diseases such as *E. coli* 0157 (VTEC) cause a range of illnesses from mild non-bloody diarrhoea to haemorrhagic colitis. Most illnesses are self-limiting and resolve within seven days, however simple steps such as hand washing can quickly control the risks from farm visits.

## Before visiting the farm

It is always useful to discuss the visiting arrangements with the farm management and check that the facilities available are the same as those described in the Health and Safety Executive (HSE 2000) safety leaflet AIS23 information sheet.

### *Pregnant women*

Pregnant women should avoid accompanying the group on a farm visit as contact with farm animals at certain times (i.e. lambs in spring) has been linked to miscarriage.

### *Advice to parents*

When providing information to parents about a farm visit they need to be asked that their children wear appropriate clothing for the weather and for the time of year and that they include a change of clothing. Sturdy outdoor shoes (not sandals) or wellington boots should be worn by children if possible, as it is important because farms are working areas.

*How to prepare the children for the visit*

Before visiting the farm, staff should talk to the children about the day and what rules need to be followed regarding touching the animals, washing their hands and where they will be eating.

## During the visit

On the day of the visit adults and children should follow good hygienic practices.

It is important to remember:

+ Children are the responsibility of the early years setting staff throughout the visit.

+ Children must be supervised throughout the visit, especially when washing their hands to make sure they do it properly (farm staff may be able to help).

+ Plenty of time should be allowed before eating and leaving the farm so that the children are not rushed and therefore do not wash their hands.

+ If subsequently a child has any signs and symptoms of illness, such as sickness and diarrhoea, they should be taken to see their doctor who should be told that they have recently been on a farm visit.

## General advice

General advice for farm visits includes the following:

+ Wash and dry your hands thoroughly after touching an animal.

+ Do not eat or drink anything at all while going around the farm; only eat when away from the animals after thoroughly washing your hands.

+ Do not put your face against an animal and do not put hands into your mouth after touching an animal.

+ Do not touch animal droppings and wash your hands thoroughly immediately if you do.

+ Clean your shoes after leaving the farm, or when you get home, and then wash your hands thoroughly.

## Coastal visits

Trips to the coast can be a popular choice especially for those early years settings that are near to the sea. Awareness of the risks associated with such trips need to be recognised, linked to other activities that might be considered, such as walking on the beach and rock pooling.

In addition to the general rules when organising and planning outings and trips, the following points should be considered:

+ Obtain advice from the local coastguard, harbour master, lifeguard or tourist information office who will be able to provide information on the local area.

+ Be aware of warning signs and flags.

+ Keep away from sewage outlets and areas of beaches that are not for the general access.

+ Know the times of local tides.

+ Be aware of the dangers of paddling in the sea for young children.

## Best practice checklist

+ Check the place you want to visit before you take the children.

+ Check whether the place you want to go to has suitably qualified staff and what are the hazards of the venue.

+ Get consent forms from parents for the visit.

+ Tell the children about the outing and give instructions appropriate to their age.

+ Make sure you have the right staff to child ratio.

+ Make sure that any equipment or luggage taken is stored securely on the vehicle.

+ Have a list of emergency contacts for everyone who is going on the trip.

+ Have emergency procedures in place, especially for getting in touch with families and if the trip is late returning.

+ Identify who will be responsible for what on the trip before you go.

+ Know what the cancellation arrangements will be.

+ Check what transport arrangements have been made.

+ Provide information to parents, staff and volunteers about the visit.

---

**SELF-REVIEW ACTIVITY**

Plan an outing suitable for a group of three-year-olds that would contribute to their development and utilise areas of the early years curriculum. Evaluate the plan and its implementation.

You may consider:

+ venue

+ the time of year

+ staff to child ratio

+ appropriate clothing

+ learning activities

+ advice to parents

+ emergency contact details

+ transport

+ parental consent.

---

## End-of-chapter summary

All children must be kept safe on outings while being encouraged to explore their environment. To achieve this the principles of safety awareness are important along with anticipating hazards that might be encountered. This chapter has stressed the need for planning and organisation and the suitability of the location for young children.

## CHAPTER 5

# What to do in cases of injury

## Introduction

While most accidents that happen to young children occur in and around the home, accidents can and do happen to children wherever they are cared for. Early years settings, under the Health and Safety at Work etc. Act (1974) and subsequent legislation, are required to provide a safe environment not only for children in their care but also for their staff and for visitors who may come onto their premises. This chapter looks at the most common types of accidents that happen in the workplace, providing information about accidents that children under the age of five years are most at risk of suffering and how to prevent them. Also included is an introduction to first aid for such injuries, a self-review activity and best practice checklist.

## Type of accidents

For children over the age of one year accidental injury is the biggest single cause of death in the UK and in 2002, 320 children under the age of 15 years died because of an injury or poisoning (CAPT 2003). The majority of these accidents are due to falls by children either slipping or tripping on the same level, such as on a pavement or on a rug. Babies and young children are also sometimes hurt after falling from one level to another, such as from a chair, bed or changing table onto the floor or on or from the stairs.

In children, scalds happen more often than burns and are mostly due to hot drinks. House fires cause the most accidental deaths of children, with 32 children dying in 2002.

While the majority of suspected poisoning cases in children needed little or no further treatment, in 2002, over 26,000 children under five years were taken to hospital after a suspected poisoning.

## Common types of accidents

### Trips and falls

Children slip and lose their grip or their balance when playing and are hurt not only by falling off the play equipment, but also by hitting themselves on the equipment as they fall. Colliding with other children and also hitting fixed or moving equipment are also common causes of injury. Over 75 per cent of accidents that happen to children in play areas are due to falls. Less common types of accidents include:

+ cuts and crush injuries when a child comes into contact with protrusions, pinch points and sharp edges on equipment;

+ strangulation when children's clothing, especially scarves, drawstrings or cords, catches on equipment;

+ entrapment injuries when the head or shoulders become stuck.

It is important to remember that even very young babies, while they might not be mobile, can wriggle, kick or roll into situations that could become hazardous such as rolling off the bed, work surface or changing table. Once babies start crawling they can start to climb onto furniture and windowsills. If furniture is not stable there is always the risk of injury from it tipping over or moving if it has wheels. Anchoring heavy items of furniture to the wall, moving beds and chairs to remove access to windows to prevent children climbing up and falling, and fitting window locks or safety catches that stop the window opening more than 2.5 inches (6.5 cm) all help to reduce the risk of injuries.

Finally, to reduce the risk of injuries on the stairs, fit safety gates at the top and bottom of the stairs.

### Cuts and abrasions

With the increased use of glass in modern buildings there is also an increased risk of cuts to young children. Glass is a major hazard and comes in a number of forms including ordinary glass, laminated safety glass and toughened safety glass. Ensure that any glass that is fitted complies with British Standard BS 6206 and if in doubt seek expert advice from a Glass and Glazing Federation glazier.

Having access to sharp knives, scissors, razors and gardening tools can also cause cuts.

Safe practice can be achieved by:

+ having safety glass fitted in doors and windows;

+ marking large areas of glass with stickers to let people know it is there;

+ fitting safety catches on drawers that contain sharp cutlery and knives;

+ keeping kitchen gadgets, sewing materials and gardening tools out of reach of young children;

+ replacing glass in bookcases with safety glass;

+ checking outdoor areas for broken glass, rusty nails and used drink cans etc. before children are allowed to play;

+ wrapping any glass carefully in newspaper before placing it into the bin.

Abrasions can be caused from falling and scraping knees or elbows, and while thought of as minor injuries, they do hurt and can become infected. They are easily dealt with:

+ Clean the area with warm water and soap.

+ Pat dry.

+ If there is little bleeding leave the graze uncovered.

+ If the bleeding continues cover with a sterile non-stick dressing pad.

+ If the wound continues to look inflamed or infected then contact NHS Direct or the practice nurse at your local health centre.

### Electrical shocks

Electricity kills, and approximately 1,000 accidents occur in the workplace and are reported to the Health and Safety Executive (HSE) each year. The 220 voltage of domestic electricity supply can kill or severely injure a child, causing burns unless a Residual Current Device (RCD) that cuts out the supply is fitted. All nurseries and homes should have an RCD fitted to protect everyone from incurring an accidental electric shock.

Ways of preventing such accidents include:

+ having an RCD fitted to protect the electric circuit;

+ using BEAB approved appliances;

+ fitting safety covers over electric sockets, preventing children poking anything, including their fingers, into them;

+ unplugging electrical appliances when not in use;

+ making sure flexes are connected to plugs and appliances correctly;

+ learning how to wire a plug correctly;

+ replacing worn or frayed flexes;

+ testing of all electrical appliances by a qualified electrician should be undertaken annually.

## Poisoning

Many children under the age of five are admitted to hospital every year because of unintentional poisoning: 26,000 children in the UK during 2002 went to hospital because of poisoning with six children subsequently dying, one of whom was under five years old (CAPT 2004a).

Most hospital admissions are due to swallowing medicines, with analgesics being the most common, but other medicines include tranquillisers, anti-depressants, vitamins and sleeping tablets. Other substances that children swallow and can cause harm are:

+ household and garden chemicals;

+ household products of bleach, disinfectant, dishwasher powder.

These products can cause burns to the mouth, throat, oesophagus and stomach and are highly toxic.

In addition:

+ Glues, solvents and aerosols can cause burns or sickness if they are inhaled.

+ Alcohol should be treated as a poison to young children, some mouthwashes contain alcohol.

+ Cigarettes and tobacco cause sickness if eaten.

+ Cosmetics can be poisonous to young children.

+ Perfume, nail varnish remover and hairspray can be harmful if swallowed and many have a high alcohol content.

+ Essential oils can be poisonous if swallowed.

+ Plants can have poisonous leaves, seeds or berries, examples being laburnum leaves and seeds, holly berries, lupin seeds and laurel leaves.

Because babies and young children learn about their world by touching and tasting they are likely to put things into their mouths and so are at risk of poisoning. By the time they are 18 months old toddlers can open containers and when they are three they may also be able to open child-resistant tops. Reduce access to poisonous substances and know how to respond to cases of suspected poisoning:

+ Store household chemicals and medicines away from young children in a locked cupboard.

+ Store garden and DIY products in a locked outdoor shed or cupboard.

+ Do not put medicines in the fridge – when labels say 'store in a cool place' it means away from heat and a locked medicine cabinet in the bathroom achieves this.

+ Keep all medicines and household chemicals in their original container so that they can be recognised as dangerous substances and the warning labels and instructions can be followed every time they are used.

+ While child-resistant bottles are important they are not childproof and work by *slowing down* access to dangerous substances.

+ Parents and carers should learn basic first aid for babies and young children.

+ Get advice from a doctor, hospital or NHS Direct on 0845 46 47 if a child has or is suspected of having swallowed something poisonous.

+ Do not make a child vomit, take the child to the doctor or hospital along with the bottle, packet or item that you think is the cause of the poisoning.

### Drowning

Children can drown very quickly in very little water (less than 2 inches) so all sources of water can be potentially dangerous, including garden ponds, rivers, lakes, buckets and bowls of water, bath water, puddles and bird baths.

Measures to prevent such accidents include:

+ supervising children at all times when they are in or near water;

+ never leaving young children alone in the bath for even a moment;

+ not using bath seats as they do not prevent drowning;

+ emptying the bath immediately after use;

+ draining or securely covering garden ponds;

+ not leaving items that can collect rainwater in the garden, such as buckets, wheelbarrows etc. – put them away after use.

## Burns and scalds

Around 95 per cent of all thermal injuries happen to children in the home. Such burns and scalds result in over 100,000 people every year attending hospital with their injuries, which range from minor to fatal and are due to a wide variety of causes. Just under half of these injuries happen to children under the age of five (DTI 1999).

Hot drinks are the most common single cause of scalds in children, with babies and toddlers particularly at risk from pouring cups and mugs of tea and coffee over themselves. Steam or boiling water from kettles and hot oil or fat can cause scalding and young children can also be scalded by hot water from the tap.

The burns injuries that children suffer from occur after contact with open fires, cookers, barbecues, fireworks, matches, cigarette lighters and candles.

Young children are particularly vulnerable to sunburn as their skin is very sensitive and burns easily. Babies under six months old should be kept out of the sun and after this age children should be kept out of the sun when it is at its strongest. They should be dressed in loose clothing with sunblock applied and wearing a hat that covers the back of the neck.

The following actions can prevent injuries:

+ fitting smoke alarms and checking that they work on a regular basis;

+ not holding or picking up a child with a hot drink in your hand;

+ keeping mugs away from the edges of tables and work surfaces, out of sight and reach of young children;

+ using kettles that have short or coiled flex that are out of sight and reach of young children;

+ making sure young children do not play with hot taps;

+ ensuring all hot water is delivered below 46°C to avoid scalding;

+ always running cold water into baths and sinks before adding the hot;

+ always checking the temperature of food or drink when heated in a microwave before giving it to a child;

+ remembering that barbecues remain hot for several hours after they have been used;

+ fitting fireguards to all heaters and fires including radiators;

+ not letting children play with candles or leave them burning unattended;

+ keeping matches and cigarette lighters out of sight and reach of young children.

## Toys and play equipment

Children under the age of three years are the most likely to have an accident which involves a toy either when they are playing or by tripping over them especially when they are left on stairs or steps.

High numbers of accidental injuries are associated with the following toys:

+ 5,500 accidents with cars or rocking horses

+ 4,000 accidents with toy boxes

+ 4,000 accidents with model cars, planes and trains

+ 1,500 accidents with soft toys such as teddies, dolls and action figures

+ 1,000 accidents with toys that fire objects such as guns, bows and arrows, water pistols or catapults.

(*Source:* Child Accident Prevention Trust (2004b) *Toys and Accidents Factsheet*)

Accidents involving toys can be reduced by choosing the right toy for the age of the child; most toys have on their packaging a suggested age range reflecting the age groups that the manufacturers believe will find the toy most appealing.

A warning symbol shows that a toy is not suitable for children under 36 months because it may have parts that could choke a young child.

Toys should also conform to the European Standard BS EN 71 which shows that the toy has been tested to agreed safety standards. The Lion Mark is used by members of the British Toy and Hobby Association and shows that a toy has been made to the highest standards of safety and quality.

Finally there is a legal requirement that all toys that are sold in the European Union carry a CE mark, but this is not a guarantee of quality or safety.

The toy safety code by the Department of Trade and Industry advises:

+ Buy safe toys – cheap toys are not bargains if a child is injured.

+ Buy toys that are the right age for the child – read the label and follow the guidelines. Only give toys that are appropriate to the child's age – young children can choke on small marbles, even balloons.

+ Throw away broken toys – it is not charity giving broken toys to others for them to have your accident.

+ Keep toys tidy – keep stairs and rooms tidy so that children and adults do not fall over them.

Other ideas for making sure that accidents do not happen with toys include:

+ checking that no small parts can become loose and swallowed or inhaled;

+ supervising children when they play with beads, buttons and Lego as they might put them in ears, up noses or swallow them;

+ storing toys at a safe level, never on high shelves;

+ using purpose-built storage boxes with lids that don't trap fingers or close completely trapping a child inside;

+ making sure that soft and furry toys only use fillings that are safe, with eyes firmly secured;

+ encouraging children to help tidy their toys away to prevent accidents;

+ never attaching toys with string around a baby's neck.

## Suffocation

Asphyxia, when the body is deprived of oxygen, caused by suffocation can be due to pillows, baby bedding of duvets and uncovered plastic mattresses, plastic bags and wrappings and pets overlaying a baby.

Babies are at an increased risk of suffocation if they sleep in adult beds as experts state that under eight months of age a baby is unable to roll away or crawl if they become trapped under a quilt, blanket or pillow or trapped between the bed and the wall. The risk increases when a parent has taken alcohol, recreational drugs or prescription medication that makes them drowsy. In such circumstances a parent could roll over onto the baby unaware that they have done so. Falling asleep with a baby on the sofa also increases the risk of the child being suffocated and is not advised.

Prevention of such accidents includes:

+ not using pillows, duvets, quilts and bean bags for children under one year old;

+ never using strings, ribbons or ties on very young children's clothing;

+ keeping plastic bags and clingfilms from children;

+ not sleeping with a baby in your bed or on the sofa as you may accidentally suffocate them while asleep;

+ placing a baby on their back to sleep, making sure they do not get trapped in the covers.

## Choking

Choking occurs when there is a blockage caused by a foreign body preventing the passage of air to the lungs. Blockages can be at the back of the throat, or further down in the trachea or bronchi of the lungs. Sometimes a foreign body is swallowed and gets stuck in the oesophagus causing similar symptoms to that of choking. The most common cause of choking accidents is food.

To prevent choking accidents follow safe eating tips:

✛ Do not leave babies alone with a feeding bottle or food.

✛ Closely supervise children at mealtimes.

✛ Teach children to remain seated during mealtimes.

✛ Cut food into small pieces that can not become lodged in the airways.

✛ Teach children not to talk or laugh when they have a mouthful of food.

✛ Teach children to chew their food slowly and thoroughly and to put only as much food into their mouths as they can chew comfortably.

Other causes of choking include:

✛ coins, marbles, watch batteries

✛ household items, pen caps, plastic bottle caps, buttons

✛ toys and uninflated balloons.

## First aid

Accidents can happen at any time, especially for young children, who have a number of bumps, falls and scratches. The majority of these incidents will be minor but some will need professional medical attention and may cause serious injury.

Consideration needs to be given not only to the children who come to your nursery but also to the staff who work there and any visitors to the premises including parents, siblings and contractors.

The important issue is that those who have an injury or become ill receive immediate attention, and serious cases are identified and the emergency services called where necessary. First aid at work guidelines (HSE, 1997) covers the arrangements that must be in place to make sure this happens. It saves lives and prevents minor injuries becoming major ones.

The aim of all first aid is to:

+ preserve life

+ limit injuries.

The minimum first-aid provision in any workplace is:

+ a suitably stocked first-aid box

+ an appointed person to be in charge of first-aid arrangements.

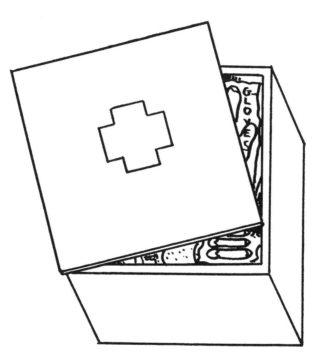

A minimum first-aid box would include:

+ A leaflet giving general advice on first aid.

+ Twenty individually wrapped sterile adhesive dressings of assorted sizes.

+ Two sterile eye pads.

+ Four individually wrapped triangular bandages.

+ Six safety pins.

+ Six medium-sized individually wrapped sterile unmedicated wound dressings.

+ Two large sterile individually wrapped unmedicated wound dressings.

+ One pair of disposable gloves.

First-aid boxes should not include medicines or tablets.

## Preventing accidents

The location and design of a play area can have an impact on child safety.

+ The layout must make sure that activities in one area do not interfere with other areas.

+ Areas for younger children must be clearly separated from those for older children.

+ Paths must be clear of equipment areas.

+ Clear sight lines throughout the play area make it easier to supervise children.

+ There should be safe access for children with special needs.

+ Lighting must be bright enough to allow for safe supervision.

The type of equipment and level of maintenance are also important factors in the number of accidents that happen.

### Minor injuries and near misses

Minor incidents can happen often, with young children frequently falling over and bumping into equipment or people. Injuries such as cuts, grazes and bruises can quickly be dealt with without much disruption, but they are also ideal opportunities to reflect on what might have happened and to be considered as near misses as part of the risk assessment process. It can be a useful learning opportunity to look at what is a minor injury, such as a fall from a climbing frame, and consider the worst-case scenario that could have occurred. Any changes to the play area can then be made before a serious accident happens.

## Serious accidents

You should always be prepared to deal with a serious injury either to a child or an adult on your premises. The injured person should be dealt with immediately:

✚ Keep the area clear around the person.

✚ Inform staff to keep children away from the area.

✚ Seek immediate medical assistance if the injury is severe or take the person to hospital.

✚ Contact the individual's family at the same time as getting medical assistance.

✚ Send a member of staff to hospital with a child so that they can explain the circumstances of the accident.

If you have to leave your early years setting to attend hospital with an injured child you should consider:

✚ Who will care for the children?

✚ Is the adult:child ratio still acceptable in your absence?

✚ Is anyone able to come in at short notice to help?

✚ If you work on your own who can you leave any remaining children with?

You should call an ambulance and not move the person if:

✚ you think they may have a back or neck injury or any injury that may become worse by movement;

✚ they are in shock and need your constant attention;

✚ they have severe chest pain or breathlessness;

✚ they have a head injury with bleeding, drowsiness or vomiting;

✚ they have loss of consciousness;

✚ they have broken bones;

✚ they have severe abdominal pain that will not go away.

## First-aid for unconsciousness

First-aid advice from the British Red Cross states that if someone looses consciousness, they need to be placed in a safe position (recovery position) to help their breathing and prevent them from choking if they should vomit.

The sequence of actions that need to be taken for a serious accident should be:

+ Make the area safe.

+ Review the situation and decide immediate priorities.

+ Check the child's responsiveness.

+ Make a conscious child comfortable and offer reassurance.

+ If unconscious and breathing place the child in the recovery position and get someone to dial 999 (or 112).

+ Maintain the airway (A).

+ Maintain the breathing (B).

+ Assess for signs of circulation by checking the pulse (C).

+ Check for and treat any severe bleeding.

+ Treat severe burns and scalds.

+ Get help.


### Recovery position for a young baby

Placing a child or adult in the 'recovery position' keeps their airway open and reduces the risk of further injury. However, for a young baby less than a year old it is not appropriate and a modified position has to be adopted.

+ Hold the baby on their side in your arms or on your lap with their head tilted down to prevent them from choking or inhaling vomit.

+ Keep a check on their breathing and pulse until the emergency services help arrives.

### Recovery position for a child

For anyone over the age of a year who is unconscious but breathing you should:

+ Turn them onto their side.

+ Lift their chin forward to open their airway.

+ Check that they cannot roll forwards or backwards.

+ Monitor their breathing and pulse.

+ If a spinal injury is suspected, use the jaw thrust technique by placing your hands on either side of the face and lifting the jaw with your fingertips to open the airway, taking care not to tilt their neck.

### Resuscitation for a baby or child

For any baby that is less than one year old you should:

+ Make sure the airway is open.

+ Place the lips over the baby's mouth and nose.

+ Blow gently into the lungs, looking along the chest as you breathe. Fill your cheeks with air and use this amount each time.

+ As the chest rises, stop blowing and allow it to fall.

+ Repeat once more then check the pulse.

+ If the pulse is still present continue Rescue Breaths for one minute then contact the emergency services by dialling 999 (or 112).

+ If the pulse is not present start chest compressions (CPR).

+ Check the pulse after every 20 breaths.

+ If the breathing starts, place the baby in the recovery position.

For a child between one and seven years of age you should:

+ Make sure the airway is open.

+ Place the lips over the child's mouth while pinching their nose.

+ Blow gently into the lungs, looking along the chest as you breathe. Take shallow breaths and do not empty your lungs completely.

+ As the chest rises, stop blowing and allow it to fall.

+ Repeat once more then check the pulse.

+ If the pulse is present continue Rescue Breaths for one minute then contact the emergency services by dialling 999 (or 112).

+ If the pulse is not present start chest compressions (CPR).

+ Check the pulse after every 20 breaths.

+ If the breathing starts place the child in the recovery position.

## Resuscitation for an adult

Anyone aged over eight years old is considered as an adult and you should:

+ Make sure the airway is open.

+ Pinch the nose firmly to close it.

+ Place the lips over the mouth and blow to make the chest rise.

+ Stop blowing and allow the chest to fall.

+ Repeat once more then check the pulse.

+ If there is no pulse start chest compressions (CPR).

+ Check the pulse after every 10 breaths.

+ If the breathing starts, place them into the recovery position.

+ Contact the emergency services by dialling 999 (or 112).

## First aid for severe bleeding

If a child has an accident that results in severe bleeding, it is important to control this as it results in reduced circulation and they may die from loss of blood.

+ Wearing disposable gloves, remove the child's clothing to expose the wound.

+ If the wound is clean of any objects, apply direct pressure to the wound using a sterile dressing pad.

+ If there is any object such as glass etc. in the wound, do not press down on the wound but apply sterile dressing pads to either side of the wound.

+ If possible elevate the injured area to slow down the flow of blood to the wound.

+ Do not remove any object that is sticking out of the wound as this could increase the bleeding.

+ Lie the injured child down and elevate the legs to reduce the risk of shock and protect them from the cold by covering them with a blanket until the emergency services arrive.

+ If blood soaks through the original dressing do not remove it but apply another dressing on top.

## First aid for wounds and bleeding

+ Bruises normally resolve themselves but applying a cold compress can relieve any pain and swelling.

+ If a child has haemophilia or other clotting disorder, they may need medical attention.

+ Clots are part of the body's normal healing process and should not be removed.

+ Small amounts of blood can go a long way, so always reassure a child and tell them what is wrong and how it is going to be fixed.

## First aid for sprains, dislocations and fractures

### Sprains

A sprain is a traumatic injury to the tendons, muscles or ligaments around a joint and is identified by the pain, swelling and discolouration seen on the skin over the joint. How long the symptoms last depends upon the amount of damage to the tissues.

Treat the area by:

+ elevating the limb to reduce swelling and strain on the area;

+ supporting the area, e.g. put the arm in a sling;

+ applying a cold compress to relieve the pain and reduce swelling (packs of cold peas from the freezer can be wrapped over the knee, ankle or elbow joint).

## Dislocations

A dislocation is when a joint is displaced from its normal position and usually happens to the shoulder, thumb or finger. It is very painful and the joint will seem abnormal.

Treat by:

✚ supporting the injured area using a sling;

✚ taking the child to hospital immediately;

✚ never trying to replace the bone back into its socket;

✚ explaining what has happened to the child and how they will make it better at the hospital.

## Fractures

A fracture of the bone is when it is broken due to a traumatic injury and is described by the part of the bone that is affected and the type of break. In young children, because their bones are still growing and are supple they break only under very severe force but are more likely to bend or crack. A common term that is used is a 'green stick fracture'. If you think a child has a fracture:

✚ Give lots of comfort and reassurance and persuade them to stay still.

✚ Do not move them unless you have to.

✚ Steady and support the injured limb with your hands to stop any movement.

✚ If there is bleeding, press a sterile pad over the wound to control the flow of blood and apply a bandage on and around the wound.

✚ If you think the leg is broken, place some padding between the knees and ankles and make a splint to stop any further movement by gently, but firmly, bandaging the good leg to the bad one at the knees and ankles, then above and below the injury.

✚ If the arm has been broken, improvise a sling to support the arm close to the body.

✚ Call the emergency services by dialling 999 (or 112).

✚ Do not give anything to eat or drink in case an operation is necessary.

✚ Watch out for signs of shock. If they become unconscious then start resuscitation.

## First aid for poisoning

✚ Children may swallow tablets, alcohol or cleaning products or eat plants that have poisonous berries or fungi.

✚ Never make a child vomit as whatever they have swallowed may be corrosive and this could cause internal injuries.

✚ If they have already vomited, try to keep a sample of the vomit to take to the hospital, or some vomit-stained clothing, as it may help the doctors to identify exactly what has been swallowed.

✚ Take any medicine bottles or plant samples to the hospital also.

✚ Never assume that the amount swallowed is too little to do any harm, always take the child to hospital.

## First-aid for foreign objects

✚ Children may place objects in their nose, ear or other parts of the body that may get stuck.

✚ You should never try to remove them as you could make the situation worse.

✚ Take the child to the nearest accident and emergency department at the local hospital where the object can be removed safely.

✚ If it affects the child's breathing explain what is happening and that they should breath through the mouth until the object has been removed by the doctor.

## First aid for febrile convulsions

✚ Febrile convulsions are fits that occur in children aged from six months to five years old, usually due to infection or inflammation of the central nervous system.

✚ Simple febrile convulsion last less than 10–15 minutes.

✚ Complex febrile convulsions last about 15–30 minutes.

✚ It is not known what causes the febrile convulsions but the most common sources of fever in children are viral infections and otitis media (infection of the middle ear).

✚ Febrile convulsions do recur but only in 30 per cent of children, mostly within a year of the first fit and to children under 15 months old.

✚ It is rare for children to develop epilepsy because of having a febrile convulsion.

✚ Immunisation rarely causes febrile convulsions.

✚ Most children do not need to go to hospital.

Controlling high temperatures can be achieved by:

✚ removing excessive clothing and bedding to cool the child down;

✚ giving medicine such as paracetamol or ibuprofen, following medical advice, to reduce the fever.

Actions such as fanning, cold bathing and tepid sponging are no longer advised as they are of little benefit.

To manage a convulsion:

+ place the child in the recovery position;

+ do not force anything into the mouth;

+ make a note of the time the convulsion starts;

+ when the convulsions stop contact the GP or NHS Direct;

+ if the convulsions last for more than five minutes contact the emergency services by dialling 999 (or 112).

### First aid for choking for a baby less than one year old

+ Place the baby's head lower than their chest with the airway in an open position.

+ Sit on a chair with the baby's face down on your lap, letting their head and chest hang down over your knees and supporting their face and neck with one hand.

+ Use the heel of your other hand to gently but firmly thump them between their shoulder blades no more than five times.

+ Do not use as much force as you would with an adult but remember you are trying to dislodge an object.

+ If this fails to dislodge the object, proceed to chest thrusts.

+ Turn the child onto their back with their head lower than their chest and the airway in an open position.

+ Place two fingers onto the breastbone (sternum) and give five chest thrusts at about one every three seconds.

+ Check the mouth after five back and five chest thrusts.

+ Carefully remove any visible foreign objects.

+ Call an ambulance if this is unsuccessful.

### First aid for choking for a child between one and eight years old

+ Encourage them to cough.

+ Remove any obvious obstruction from the mouth with your finger but do not attempt to clear debris from the back of the throat as you could push it further in.

+ Help gravity by putting the head lower than the chest by getting the child to bend forward if possible.

+ Thump them firmly between their shoulder blades with the heel of your hand no more than five times.

+ Check the mouth to see if the obstruction has been dislodged.

+ If not give five more thumps.

+ Call an ambulance if this is unsuccessful.

For any baby or young child who is choking, the best way to clear an obstruction if they are coughing effectively is to let them cough.

## First aid for burns

+ Immediately run cold water over the area for at least ten minutes.

+ Never rub butter, oil or ointment into a burn.

+ Remove any tight belts or jewellery (especially rings) that the person is wearing as burned skin can swell.

+ Cover the burned area with clingfilm or a clean smooth cloth (such as a pillowcase) to keep out infection until it can be properly dressed.

+ Unless the burn is very small go to hospital.

+ If the burn is very serious or the person is (or was) unconscious dial 999 (or 112).

+ Do not give the injured person anything to eat or drink after the accident as they may need an anaesthetic at hospital.

## Reporting of accidents

A record of all accidents should be kept no matter how minor or trivial they may seem. You should have an accident and incident report book in which entries should be made as soon as possible after the injury has occurred while it is still fresh in the mind. Certain incidents must be reported to the government agency RIDDOR. These are:

+ deaths

+ major injuries

- accidents resulting in over three-day injury
- diseases
- dangerous occurrences
- gas incidents.

To report an incident of this type you can call them on 0845 3009923 or fill in a form on their website: www.riddor.gov.uk.

Any follow-up action after a specific accident or incident should be recorded in your report book so that it can be shown that steps have been taken to prevent similar incidents reoccurring. Once an accident book is full it should be kept indefinitely in case of future claims.

### Emergency planning form

(Example of form for contacting emergency services)

Request for an ambulance to [name of premises]

Dial 999 (or 112), ask for ambulance and be ready with the following information.

1. Your telephone number

2. Your location [full address and postcode]

3. Exact location in the premises [state room e.g. baby room]

4. Your name

5. Brief description of child's symptoms.

Inform Ambulance Control of the best entrance and state that the crew will be met and taken to [name location]

Speak clearly and slowly and be ready to repeat information if asked.

(*Source:* adapted from *Managing Medicines in schools and Early Years Settings.* Department of Education and Skills 2005)

# Best practice checklist

✚ Fit safety equipment such as locks to cupboards and windows, covers for electricity sockets and safety gates to prevent access to stairs.

✚ Keep a record of all accidents.

✚ Staff should be trained in a first-aid course recognised by the Health and Safety Executive (HSE) specifically for babies and young children. The vocational level 2 paediatric first-aid course on the National Training Framework is frequently used.

✚ Have sufficient first-aid boxes relevant to the size of the nursery.

✚ Check the contents of the first-aid boxes to make sure they are complete, intact and in date.

✚ Check fire safety equipment on a regular basis.

✚ Keep and maintain records of parents contact numbers.

✚ Contact parents when a child has an accident, no matter how minor.

✚ Keep contact numbers of the emergency services, local GP, NHS Direct near the telephone.

✚ Keep all medicines, household and garden chemicals and cleaning products locked up and away from children.

✚ Only purchase toys that are appropriate to the children's age and that conform to European Standard BS EN 71.

✚ Check toys regularly to make sure that those that are broken are thrown away.

**SELF-REVIEW ACTIVITY**

Consider the areas of the nursery that children have access to and, sitting down on the floor, get a child's eye view of their world and the interesting things they can see, touch and climb.

You might include:

+ electric sockets

+ door handles

+ table corners

+ chairs to climb

+ gaps in railings and banisters to squeeze through (small children can get their bodies through gaps as small as 4 inches (10 cm) wide but their heads get trapped).

## End-of-chapter summary

As children explore their environment accidents happen. Prevention can be helped by using appropriate safety equipment to reduce the number of accidents. Items such as toys can be hazardous if they are inappropriate to the child's age, along with other play equipment and the environment. Maintaining a high adult to child ratio allows for close observation and supervision to prevent accidents from suffocation, choking, burns, scalds etc. While knowledge of first aid is essential when considering the safety of young children, the first-aid information in this chapter provides an introduction to the subject but cannot replace a first-aid course.

# Bibliography

Bilton, H. (2004) *Playing Outside: activities, ideas and inspiration for the Early Years*. London: David Fulton Publishers.

British Standard EN 1176 (1997) *The European Standard for Playground Equipment*. London: The Stationery Office.

British Standard EN 1177 (1997) *The European Standard for Impact absorbing playground surfacing: Safety requirements and test methods*. London: The Stationery Office.

Calloway, G. (2005) *The Early Years Curriculum: A View From Outdoors*. London: David Fulton Publishers.

Child Accident Prevention Trust (CAPT) (2003) *Preventing Childhood Accidents: Guidance on Effective Action*. London: CAPT. Available at www.capt.org.uk [accessed 30 March 2005]

Child Accident Prevention Trust (CAPT) (2004a) *Safety in Day Care and Play Settings*. London: CAPT. Available at www.capt.org.uk [accessed 30 March 2005]

Child Accident Prevention Trust (CAPT) (2004b) *Toys and Accidents Factsheet*. London: CAPT. Available at www.capt.org.uk [accessed 30 March 2005]

Department for Education and Skills (DfES) (1996) *Supporting pupils with medical needs in school* [online]. Circular number 14/96. Available at www.dfes.gov.uk/publications/guidanceandthelaw/14_96/summary.htm [accessed 3 January 2005]

Department for Education and Skills (1998) *Health and Safety of pupils on Educational Visits: A Good Practice Guide* (HASPEV). Available at www.dfes.gov.uk/h_s_ev/index.shtml [accessed 3 December 2004]

Department for Education and Skills (DfES) (2003) *Full Day Care: National Standards for under 8s Day Care and Childminding*. Nottingham: Surestart, DfES.

Department for Education and Skills (2005) *Managing Medicines in Schools and Early Years Settings*. London: HMSO.

Department of Education (1993) *DENI Circular 1993/2 Animals and Plants in Schools: Legal aspects*. Available at www.deni.gov.uk [accessed 30 March 2005]

Department of Health (1990) *The Children Act 1989*. London: Department of Health.

Department of Trade and Industry (1999) *Burns and Scolds Accidents in the Home*. Available at www.dti.gov.uk [accessed 30 December 2004]

Department of Trade and Industry (1990) *Toys (Safety) Regulations* (Statutory Instrument 1989 no 1275). Available at www.dti.gov.uk [accessed 30 March 2005]

Health and Safety Commission (HSC) (1999) *Management of Health and Safety at Work Act Regulations 1999*. London: HMSO.

Health and Safety Executive (HSE) (1992) *Personal Protective Equipment at Work Regulations*. London: HMSO.

Health and Safety Executive (HSE) (1995) *The Reporting of Injuries, Diseases and Dangerous Occurrences Regulations*. London: HMSO.

Health and Safety Executive (HSE) (1997) *First aid at work, your questions answered*. Sudbury: HSE. Available at www.hsebooks.co.uk [accessed 30 March 2005]

Health and Safety Executive (HSE) (2000) *Avoiding ill health at open farms – Advice to teachers* (AIS23 Supplement (revised)). Sudbury: HSE. Available at www.hsebooks.co.uk [accessed 30 March 2005]

Health and Safety Executive (HSE) (2002) *Control of Substances Hazardous to Health (COSHH) amendments Regulations 2002*. London: HSE Books.

Health and Safety Executive/Local Authorities Enforcement Liaison Committee (HELA) (2002) Local authority Circular (LAC 79/2) *Safety in Children's Playgrounds*. Sudbury, HSE. Available at http://www.hse.gov.uk/lau/lacs/79-2.htm#top [accessed 30 March 2005]

Health Service Advisory Committee (HSAC) (1974) *Health and Safety at Work etc. Act*. London: HMSO.

Macintyre, C. and McVitty, K. (2003) *Planning the Pre-5 Setting*. London: David Fulton Publishers.

Morrison, G. (2001) 'Zoonotic infections from pets: understanding the risks and treatments'. *Postgraduate Medicine,* 110(1), July.

Public Health Laboratory Service (PHLS) Advisory Committee on Gastrointestinal Infections (2000) 'Guidelines for the control of infection with Vero cytotoxin producing *Escherichia coli* (VTEC)'. *Communicable Disease and Public Health,* 3, 14–23.

Resuscitation Council (UK) (2000a) *Resuscitation Guidelines 2000* [online]. Available at http://www.resus.org.uk/pages/guideint.htm [accessed 06/04/2005]

Resuscitation Council (UK) (2000) *Newborn Life Support Resuscitation Guidelines 2000* [online]. Available at http://www.resus.org.uk/pages/guideint.htm [accessed 06/04/2005]

Royal Horticultural Society (2004) *Potentially Harmful Garden Plants.* Surrey: RHS. Available at www.rhs.org.uk/publications [accessed 30 March 2005]

Royal Society for the Prevention of Accidents *Home and Garden Safety Checklist.* Available at www.rospa.co.uk [accessed 27 February 2005]

St John Ambulance (2005) *First aid advice online – the primary survey.* Available at http://www.sja.org.uk/firstaid/info/primarySurvey.asp [accessed 02/03/2005]

# Index

# More Early Years titles available from...

**David Fulton** Publishers

## Developing Play for the Under 3s
The Treasure Basket and Heuristic Play

**Anita M. Hughes**

The Treasure Basket and Heuristic
Play promote extraordinary capacities of concentration, intellectual brilliance and manipulative mastery for babies and young children.

The approach appears deceptively simple: offering natural and household objects to babies and toddlers can transform their learning. It is based on much more complicated research into how babies learn, the principles of learning, research evidence and the author's own personal experience of working with the under 3s. The book provides:

• A new approach to understanding and providing for play and learning for the under 3s

• Explanations about what babies do and how this links with later conceptual thinking

• Ideas and activities for use in the nursery or at home.

£12 • Paperback • 112 pages • 1-84312-429-7 • March 2006

## Understanding the Reggio Approach
Reflections on the Early Childhood Experience of Reggio Emilia

**Linda Thornton and Pat Brunton**

A much needed source of information for those wishing to extend and consolidate their understanding of the Reggio Approach, this book:

• Analyses the essential elements of the Reggio Approach to early childhood

• Provides examples from the infant toddler centres and preschools to illustrate these elements

• Focuses upon the key ideas that practitioners should consider when reviewing and reflecting on their practice

• Can be used as a basis for continuing professional development and action research.

Written to support the work of all those in the field of early education and childcare, this is a vital text for students, early years and childcare practitioners, teachers, advisory teachers, setting managers and headteachers.

£16 • Paperback • 114 pages • 1-84312-241-3 • January 2005

## Feeding the Under 5s

**Allan Dyson and Lucy Meredith**

One young child in every four is overweight, and one in ten is obese. Among the reasons for this are a general lack of interest and understanding in food and cooking, junk food being consumed every day and a more sedentary school life. This is an issue that needs to be tackled early starting with the under 5s. This book offers:

• Advice and recipe ideas for feeding young children properly

• Ways of improving young children's understanding of food and nutrition

• Contemporary evidence and policies recommended by expert advisory bodies

• Underlying reasons behind nutritional guidelines and food safety advice and practical ways to implement them.

£17 • Paperback • 96 pages • 1-84312-388-6 • June 2006

## The New Early Years Professional

**Edited by Angela Nurse**

Celebrating the spirit and need for increased multi-disciplinary working and co-operation in the care and education of children, this book addresses the emergence of a new type of early years professional. It will support the reader in understanding the background and context of the current situation of change and excitement, as well as helping them reflect on the challenges and possibilities of future early years and interagency working. It covers key issues such as:

• Families, children and culture

• Health and well-being

• Safeguarding children

• Leadership and management.

Adopting an analytical and reflective style appropriate for degree-level study, this book is a core reader for all Early Childhood Studies and Early Years Courses.

£18 • Paperback • 220 pages • 1-84312-423-8 • August 2006

Ordering your books couldn't be easier! See next page for details or visit www.fultonpublishers.co.uk

## Baby and Toddler Development Made Real

Featuring the Progress of Jasmine Maya 0-2 Years

**Sandy Green**

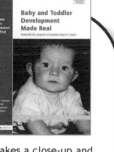

Featuring baby Jasmine, Sandy Green takes a close-up and detailed look at baby development from pre-birth to two years. This book is designed to support and consolidate understanding of how babies develop up to the age of two years. The book includes sections on:

• Pre-natal influences on post-natal development

• Pre-natal screenings and scans

• A real baby's birth

• The Neonatal phase

• General development.

Following the progress of a real baby, the book examines every part of baby care and development, including:

• Health and safety, immunisation

• Play, stimulation, toys and books

• Theories and theorists.

£17 ● Paperback ● 176 pages ● 1-84312-033-X ● January 2004

## Playing Outside

Activities, Ideas and Inspiration for the Early Years

**Helen Bilton**

*"Playing outside is a highly attractive book with more than 100 inspirational photographs and clear text...The highlighted resources, ideas, things to remember, case studies and questions to ask throughout the book make it easy to dip into, but I recommend reading it cover to cover!"*
Foundation Stage File, May 2005

Packed with all you need to know about how to make outdoor play work in practice. This book, written by the author of *Outdoor Play in the Early Years*, provides clear and detailed guidance on every aspect of outdoor play, including:

• Activities that cover all areas of learning

• Photographs illustrating good practice and imaginative use of equipment

• Examples of work from a range of settings

• Help and advice on suppliers of equipment.

This book will also help those working in schools, nurseries and pre-school units to increase the success of their outdoor play areas.

£16 ● Paperback ● 104 pages ● 1-84312-067-4 ● January 2004

# How to order from David Fulton Publishers:

Our books are available from your usual supplier, but if it is more convenient, you can order directly from us.

**1** Tel:     0845 602 1937

**2** Fax:     0845 601 5358

**3** Post:    David Fulton Publishers
         The Chiswick Centre
         414 Chiswick High Road
         London
         W4 5TF

**4** Email:   orders@fultonpublishers.co.uk

**5** Web:     www.fultonpublishers.co.uk

Free P&P to schools, LEAs and other organisations

£2.50 per order for private/personal orders